Food Chains and Webs

Holly Wallace

Heinemann Library
Chicago, Illinois

Customer Service 888-454-2279

Visit our website at www.heinemannlibrary.com

Designed by Celia Floyd
Originated by Dot Gradations
Printed in China by Wing King Tong

05 04 03

10 9 8 7 6 5 4 3 2

Library of Congress Cataloging-in-Publication Data

Wallace, Holly, 1961-
  Food chains and webs / Holly Wallace.
     p. cm. -- (Life processes)
  Includes bibliographical references (p.).
  ISBN 1-57572-338-7 (HC), 1-4034-4074-3 (Pbk.)
   1. Food chains (Ecology)--Juvenile literature. [1. Food chains (Ecology) 2. Ecology.] I.
Title. II. Series.

  QH541.14 .G35 2000
  577'.16--dc21

                                                                    00-040939

Acknowledgments

The author and publishers are grateful to the following for permission to reproduce copyright material: Bruce Coleman Collection/Jeff Foott, p. 10; Bruce Coleman Collection/Sir Jeremy Grayson, p. 26; Bruce Coleman Collection/Andrew Purcell, p. 19; NHPA/B. & C. Alexander, p. 24; NHPA/Mark Bowler, p. 17; NHPA/Laurie Campbell, p. 22; NHPA/Nigel J. Dennis, p. 8; NHPA/Martin Harvey, p. 13; NHPA/T. Kitchin & V. Hurst p. 13; NHPA/Hellio & Van Ingen, p. 28; NHPA/Ralph & Daphne Keller, p. 4; NHPA/Michael Leach, p. 9; NHPA/Rod Planck, p. 5; NHPA/Jany Sauvanet, p. 11; NHPA/Kevin Schafer, p. 12; NHPA/B. Jones & M. Shimlock, p. 23; NHPA/R. Sorensen & J. Olsen, p. 29; NHPA/Bill Wood, p. 21; Oxford Scientific Films/Daniel J. Cox, p. 15; Oxford Scientific Films/Michael Fogden, p. 16.

Cover photograph reproduced with permission of Still Pictures.

Some words are shown in bold, **like this.** You can find out what they mean by looking in the glossary.

Contents

Introduction

Food Chains and Webs looks at the way plants and animals in a particular place are connected by what they eat. Because green plants can make their own food, they begin every food chain and web. All animals, including people, rely on plants for their food. The search for food takes up much of their lives.

Food and Feeding

All living things must eat to stay alive. Food provides them with the energy they need to make new cells, to grow, and to stay healthy. Green plants are able to make their own food by **photosynthesis.** Animals cannot make their own food. They have to move around to hunt or **forage** for food. Some animals eat plants. Others eat animals that have fed on plants. In this way, all animals depend on the food stored in plants to provide them with energy for their own life processes.

The sheep grazing on grass in Australia are primary consumers.

Ecosystems and food chains

An **ecosystem** is made up of a **habitat** and the **community** of plants and animals that live in it. The plants and animals in an ecosystem react with each other and with their surroundings. They are linked to each other by their feeding habits. The energy produced by plants is passed on through the community in a food chain. Each link in the chain is food for the next living thing in line.

Some food chains are quite direct. For example, in the Arctic, sea plants are eaten by fish that are eaten by seals that are eaten by polar bears. An ecosystem can also have many different chains linked together in a complex web.

Plant producers

Because green plants can make their own food, they start off every food chain. They are eaten by animals that may, in turn, be eaten by other animals. Plants are called **producers** because they use the sun's energy to produce food. Animals that feed directly on plants are called primary **consumers.** Animals that eat primary consumers are called secondary consumers. They may themselves be eaten by tertiary consumers.

Photosynthesis

Plants make food in their leaves, which contain a special green **pigment,** or coloring, called **chlorophyll.** The chlorophyll uses energy absorbed from sunlight to convert **carbon dioxide** from the air, and water from the ground, into a simple sugary food called **glucose.** This process is called photosynthesis. **Oxygen** is given off as a waste product. The food can be stored inside the plant's leaves, stems, fruit, seeds, and roots until it is needed.

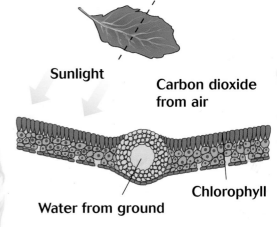

Sunlight

Carbon dioxide from air

Water from ground

Chlorophyll

Photosynthesis makes glucose from sunlight, water, and carbon dioxide.

Did you know?

Many plants have special features to protect themselves from being eaten. Cacti, for example, grow in the scorching deserts. Their stems are covered in prickly spines instead of leaves. Large leaves lose water quickly, but spines help keep water loss to a minimum and keep hungry animals away.

The giant saguaro cactus grows a new arm every 50 years.

How Food Chains Worl

The living things in a **community** are connected by
what they eat. For example, plants are eaten by snails,
which in turn may be eaten by birds. Along the way, the
energy produced by green plants is passed up the food
chain. Some food chains have more links than others. For
example, a bird may be eaten by a bigger bird or by a
fox. Animals that eat other animals are called
predators. The animals that are eaten are called **prey.**
Most **ecosystems** have plants, predators, and prey.

Food webs

Because animals often eat a variety of things, they may
appear in more than one food chain. Within an ecosystem,
these different food chains are joined to form a food web.
The food chain below is part of a larger, woodland food
web. In this food web, the **producers** are the plants and
trees. Animals such as snails and rabbits feed directly on
plants and so are primary **consumers.** Birds that eat plants
or seeds are also primary consumers. However, if the birds
eat snails or rabbits, they are secondary consumers. The fox
is a secondary consumer if it eats a seed-eating bird, but it
is a **tertiary** consumer if it eats a snail-eating bird.

A woodland
food web.

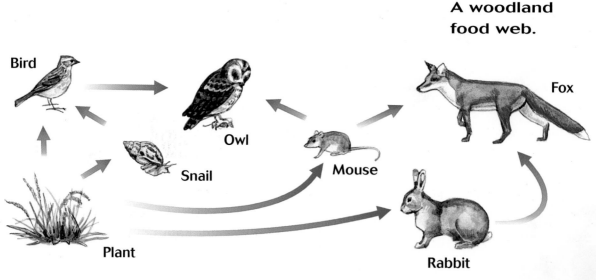

Bird

Owl

Snail

Mouse

Fox

Rabbit

Plant

6

Pyramid of numbers

The numbers of living things at each stage of a food chain can be shown using a diagram called a **pyramid of numbers.** In most ecosystems, there must be more plants than prey and more prey than predators. For example, in the food chain on the previous page, there must be more plants than snails and more snails than birds. Otherwise, neither the snails nor the birds would have enough to eat. This information can be shown like this:

This is a simple pyramid of numbers.

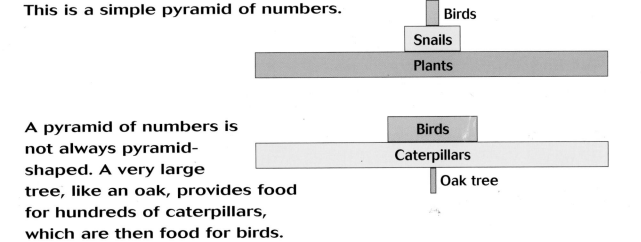

A pyramid of numbers is not always pyramid-shaped. A very large tree, like an oak, provides food for hundreds of caterpillars, which are then food for birds.

Pyramid of biomass

The **mass** of living things at each stage of a food chain can be shown using a diagram called a **pyramid of biomass.** Biomass means the total mass of each type of living thing in the food chain. The pyramid of biomass for the oak tree food chain would look like this:

The pyramid shows how huge and heavy the single oak tree is, compared to all the caterpillars and all the birds together. Its biomass is much greater than that of the caterpillars that feed on it. Likewise, the biomass of the caterpillars is much greater than that of the birds.

Herbivores

Herbivores are primary **consumers.** They are animals that live entirely on plants. They range from tiny insects that suck plant juices to huge elephants that uproot whole trees. Because the energy provided by plant food doesn't last very long, herbivores spend a large part of their lives eating just to get enough energy. They do not have to hunt for food because plants do not move around. But they often face fierce competition for food supplies from other herbivores.

These giraffes are primary consume[rs]

Grassland grazers

Grasslands around the world provide food for many different herbivores. The animals are able to live together because each one eats a different part of a plant. On the African grasslands, such animals as giraffes and elephants eat the leaves from trees and bushes. They are called **browsers.** A giraffe's long neck helps it reach leaves high up in the trees. Other animals, such as zebras and antelopes, eat grass. They are called **grazers.**

Did you know?

African elephants have enormous appetites. These huge herbivores feed for about eighteen hours a day. Their skulls, teeth, and jaws are specialized for crushing and chewing tough plant material. An adult elephant eats about 496 pounds (225 kilograms) of grass, leaves, bark, flowers, and fruit a day. Some male elephants may eat twice that much!

Eating seeds

Many birds are herbivores that eat the fruit, nuts, and seeds of plants. Their beaks are specialized to suit their diets. Finches have short, strong, sharply pointed beaks for cracking open tough seed cases and reaching the food inside. Crossbills have unusual, crossed beaks for prying seeds out of pine cones. Parrots have very strong, hooked beaks for cracking nuts. They use the hooked tips for pulling the soft pulp out of fruit.

A crossbill is adapted to eating seeds from pine cones.

Nectar drinkers

Every part of a plant—the roots, stem, leaves, and flowers—provides food for a variety of insects. Butterflies lay their eggs on plant leaves so that the caterpillars have plenty of food to eat when they hatch. Caterpillars can easily strip a plant bare. Adult butterflies suck up liquid nectar from inside a plant's flower with a long, hollow tube called a **proboscis.** The proboscis is coiled up when it is not being used.

Not being eaten

Herbivore insects are eaten by birds and other animals who are secondary consumers in the food chain. Many herbivores have developed features to avoid being eaten. Some simply fly away. Others, such as stick insects, are perfectly **camouflaged** to look like the leaves or twigs on which they feed. Some moths have eye-like markings that scare off hungry birds.

Carnivores

Meat-eating animals are called **carnivores.** They are the next link in the food chain. Carnivores are **predators**— animals that hunt other animals, which are called **prey.** Carnivores have special features for hunting and eating their prey. These may include sharp, pointed teeth and claws for gripping and tearing prey. Finding food can take a great deal of time and energy. Small carnivores, such as shrews, use up energy very quickly. They must eat their own weight in food each day; otherwise they will starve to death. In contrast, large carnivores, such as lions, need to eat much less.

Hunting in packs

Wolves are typical carnivores. They have large, dagger-like front teeth, called canines, for gripping prey. Between the canines are small, pointed incisor teeth for cutting through flesh. At the back of the wolf's mouth are its molar, or carnassial, teeth. These have sharp, scissor-like edges for slicing through tough hide, muscle, and bone.

Wolves feed mostly on large mammals such as deer and moose. They hunt in well-organized packs and follow a set plan of attack.

Anteaters

The giant anteater, shown in the picture, has a long, pointed snout and a long, sticky tongue for catching its prey of ants and termites. It tears open an ants' nest with its sharp, strong claws, then flicks its tongue in and out, lapping up hundreds of ants at a time. It needs to eat about 30,000 ants a day to get all the energy it needs.

Insect carnivores

Mammals are not the only carnivores. Many insects and fish are meat-eaters, too. Robber flies are fierce predators. They perch on twigs, then pounce on other insects that fly past. Then they suck out the insects' juices. Robber flies have hairy faces to protect their eyes from their prey, which may include stinging insects.

Scavenging for scraps

Some carnivores are **scavengers.** They eat prey that has died naturally or has been killed by another carnivore. Griffon vultures in Africa eat the remains of a lion's or cheetah's kill. They hover overhead until the lions have eaten their fill, then flock around the carcass. They can strip an antelope to the bone in just 20 minutes.

Did you know?

Some plants are carnivores. The Venus flytrap can make its own food by **photosynthesis,** but it eats meat to get extra nourishment. This unusual plant has hinged leaves that lie open as it waits for an insect to land. Then the leaves snap shut. Special digestive juices help the plant dissolve the insect's body.

Omnivores

Omnivores are animals that eat both plants and animals. They include bears, rats, pigs, chimpanzees, and human beings. Because omnivores eat a wide variety of foods, they usually have little problem finding enough to eat. If one type of food becomes scarce, omnivores can turn to another type of food. In addition, the teeth and other feeding features of omnivores do not need to be as specialized as those of **herbivores** or **carnivores.**

A varied diet

Most bears are omnivorous, taking advantage of whatever food they can find. Depending upon where they live, bears' diets include fruit, leaves, nuts, honey, small mammals, and fish. Spectacled bears from South America eat a particularly wide range of food. Their diet contains more than 80 different types of food, which include deer, birds, rabbits, fruit, flowers, cacti, orchids, and moss.

A spectacled bear feeds on leaves.

Did you know?
Cockroaches are **scavengers.** They usually feed on dead or decaying plants. In many parts of the world, cockroaches have become pests, eating anything from scraps of food in kitchens to household garbage. Cockroaches can easily spread disease.

Chimpanzee hunters

Chimpanzees eat a mixed diet, including leaves, buds, seeds, eggs, and termites. The chimpanzee in the picture is using a stick to dig for bugs to eat. But they also catch larger **prey.** Some chimpanzees are fierce hunters. They form well-organized groups to hunt for colobus monkeys or wild pigs. Any meat they catch is shared among the whole group.

City living

Omnivores have extremely adaptable feeding habits. Red foxes and coyotes are now common in many towns and cities, where they make their dens in parks and fields. They hunt rabbits, birds, and small rodents and **forage** for fruit. Some animals also raid trash cans for leftovers.

In North America, raccoons raid trash cans for people's leftovers.

Fussy eaters

The diet of the giant panda is highly specialized. Up to 95 percent of its food is made up of bamboo stems, branches, and leaves. Many different species of bamboo grow in the panda's forest home, but each panda eats only a few bamboo species. To get enough energy to survive, the panda must spend up to fifteen hours a day feeding. Pandas can digest only about a fifth of the bamboo they eat. But the panda is not a total herbivore—very occasionally it eats fish and rodents.

13

Woodland Food Chains

Woodlands and forests cover almost a third of the Earth's land surface. With plenty of trees and plants to provide food, they are the start of a great many food chains. **Temperate** forests grow between the tropics and polar regions. They have warm summers and cold winters, and contain mostly **deciduous** trees, such as oaks, maples, and sycamores. **Boreal** forests grow further north. These are huge forests of **coniferous** trees, such as pine, spruce, and fir.

Forest food web

The Eastern Mixed Forest is a great woodland region in the eastern United States. There, the boreal, coniferous forest of the north meets the temperate, deciduous forest further south. The forest contains more than 150 species of trees, including maples, beeches, and pines. These are the **producers.** A wide range of animals relies on them for food.

A North American Mixed-forest Food Web

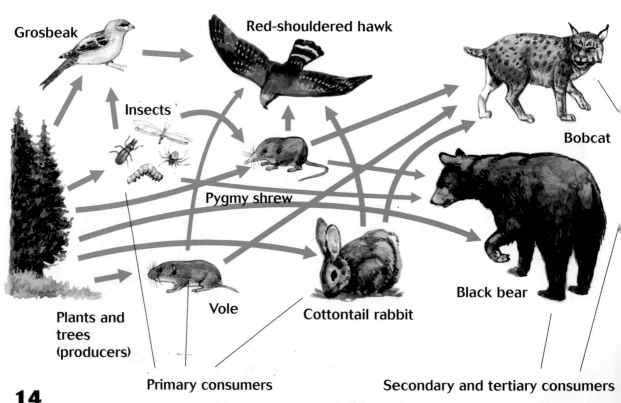

Grosbeak

Red-shouldered hawk

Insects

Bobcat

Pygmy shrew

Black bear

Plants and trees (producers)

Vole

Cottontail rabbit

Primary consumers

Secondary and tertiary consumers

Life in an oak tree

In an oak forest, a single oak tree provides shelter and food for thousands of woodland creatures. Moth caterpillars, weevils, and chafer beetles feed on the leaves. In turn, these insects provide food for birds. Acorns are eaten by birds, voles, and squirrels. Dead leaves on the ground provide food for woodlice, worms, and small mammals. Owls shelter among the branches and hunt mice and voles.

Forests in winter

In autumn, the leaves of deciduous trees change color to red, yellow, or orange. This happens as the **chlorophyll** in the leaves starts to break down, allowing other **pigments** to show through. Then the trees shed their leaves. This allows them to survive the cold winter when it is difficult to get water from the frozen ground and make food. The lack of leaves means that food is scarce for woodland **consumers.** Some, such as dormice, survive by **hibernating.** Others, such as squirrels, live on stores of nuts and acorns.

Did you know?

Koalas live in the eucalyptus forests of southeastern Australia. Eucalyptus trees are **evergreen,** providing food all year round. Koalas feed almost entirely on eucalyptus, consuming more than two pounds (907 grams) of leaves each day.

A koala feeds on eucalyptus leaves—its only food.

Rain Forest Food Chain

Although rain forests cover only about a tenth of the Earth's land surface, they are home to at least half of all the world's plants and animals. Rain forests have the highest **biomass** of any **ecosystem,** and the greatest variety of living things. Rain forests grow in layers, which are divided according to the height of the trees. Each layer has its own **community** of plants and animals and its own food chains. From the ground up, the layers are called the floor, the understory, the canopy, and the emergent layer.

Forest floor dwellers

The forest floor is dark, gloomy, and covered in a thick blanket of fallen leaves that **decompose** quickly and transfer their goodness back into the soil. The leaves provide food for insects and other creatures, such as millipedes. Millipedes burrow in the soil and leaf litter, grazing on half-decayed leaves. If they are threatened, they curl up into balls until danger passes. Small mammals feed on the insects and are **prey** for larger **predators,** such as jaguars.

Did you know?

The beautiful flower mantis is an insect perfectly **camouflaged** as a rain forest flower. The mantis' wings look like petals, which helps it surprise its prey. The animal stands on a twig, ready to shoot out its front legs and catch passing insects. Other mantises disguise themselves as twigs or leaves to avoid being eaten.

Beware–poison!

The poison-arrow frog lives in both the understory and the forest canopy. It feeds mainly on insects. To avoid being eaten itself by birds or snakes, the poison-arrow frog has deadly poisonous skin. Just one drop can kill a bird instantly. The frog's bright colors warn predators to stay away. People of the rain forest extract the poison and use it on their hunting arrows.

Monkey-eating eagles

The tallest rain forest trees form the emergent layer, up to 200 feet above the ground. Here, large birds of prey, like the monkey-eating eagle, shown in this picture, make their nests. These huge predators hunt for prey in the next layer down, the canopy, diving and twisting through the branches in search of monkeys. They take their prey back to their nests to eat.

Rain forest herbivores

Many rain forest animals live in the trees, where leaves and fruits make up a large part of their diets. An orangutan feeds mainly on rain forest fruits, such as figs, mangoes, lychees, and durian fruit. Different trees produce fruit at different times of the year. The orangutans have the amazing ability to remember which trees are in fruit at particular times and where they are.

Freshwater Food Chains

Only about three percent of all the water on Earth is freshwater. The rest is salty and makes up the seas and oceans. Fresh water is found in rivers, ponds, lakes, and marshes all over the world. Freshwater **habitats** have an **ecosystem** with its own distinctive food chains and webs. In a freshwater food chain, the **producers** are water plants. These are eaten by thousands of tiny **invertebrates,** such as insects, insect **larvae,** snails, and shrimps, which in turn provide a rich food supply for many other freshwater creatures.

Pond plants

All freshwater animals either directly or indirectly depend on plants for their food. Pond plants can be divided into three types. Marginal plants grow in zones around the edge of the pond; floating plants grow on the water; and submerged plants grow under water. The plants range from huge water lilies to microscopic **algae.** They provide not only food for the **consumers,** but also shelter and egg-laying sites for them.

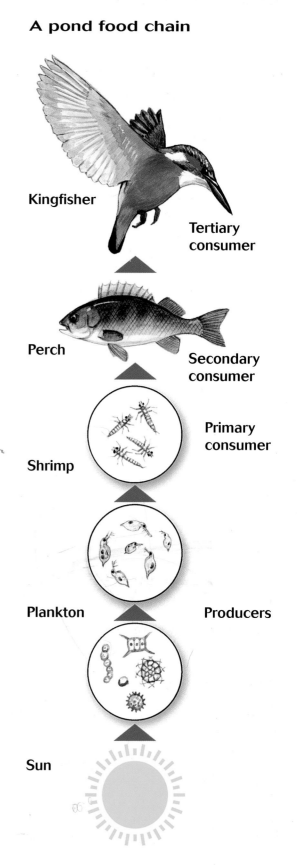

A pond food chain

Kingfisher — Tertiary consumer

Perch — Secondary consumer

Shrimp — Primary consumer

Plankton — Producers

Sun

18

Going fishing

Fish are food for many freshwater birds. Many of these birds have specially adapted feet and beaks to help them catch their food. A heron has long legs for wading in the water. It stands very still until a fish swims by, then grabs it with its long, pointed beak. A kingfisher is built for diving. It plunges into the water and stabs fish with its sharp beak.

Underwater feeding

The duck-billed platypus lives in streams, rivers, and lakes in eastern Australia. It is one of only three **species** of mammal that lay eggs. Platypuses eat insects, fish, larvae, shellfish, and worms that they scoop up from the streambed with their leathery, duck-like bill. They store the food in their cheeks until they come to the surface and eat it. Platypuses can close their eyes and ears under water to keep water out.

A dragonfly larva eats a worm.

Dragonfly diet

Insects live in every part of a freshwater ecosystem and play a vital part in the food chain. Many provide food for birds and other creatures. Some are **predators** in their own right. Adult dragonflies are skillful hunters, catching insect **prey** in mid-air. They are also fierce hunters, preying on water fleas, tadpoles, and even small fish.

Did you know?

Piranha fish live in the Amazon River in South America. These small but ferocious hunters are famous for their razor-sharp teeth. Piranhas attack their prey in **shoals,** becoming more frenzied as they feed. Their normal prey is dead or injured fish. But piranhas can strip an animal as large as a cow to its bones in just minutes. Not all piranhas are **carnivores.** Some eat fruit and leaves that fall into the water.

Ocean Food Chains

The oceans and seas form an enormous **ecosystem** that covers about two-thirds of the Earth. A huge variety of living things is found in the oceans, on the surface and at every depth. As on land, plants and animals in the ocean are connected by what they eat. There are thousands of different ocean food chains that link together to form a massive and complicated food web.

Ocean plants

As on land, every ocean food chain starts with green plants. The ocean's primary **producers** are microscopic single-celled plants called **phytoplankton.** They are **algae,** the simplest type of plants. They grow in the top 490 feet (150 meters) of the sea, where sunlight can reach them and they can make food by **photosynthesis.** Phytoplankton are grazed on by tiny **herbivores** called **zooplankton,** which, in turn, provide food for larger **consumers.** Without phytoplankton, nothing could live in the sea.

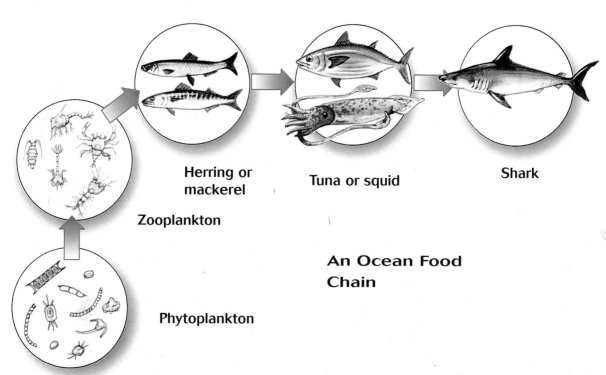

Herring or mackerel

Tuna or squid

Shark

Zooplankton

Phytoplankton

An Ocean Food Chain

Giant appetite

Some of the largest animals in the sea feed on some of the smallest. The gigantic blue whale feeds on tiny, shrimp-like creatures called krill, which are types of zooplankton. Krill live in vast **shoals.**

The blue whale filters the krill out of the seawater using long, bristly **baleen plates** that hang down from the sides of its mouth. A blue whale may eat more than 4 tons of krill a day.

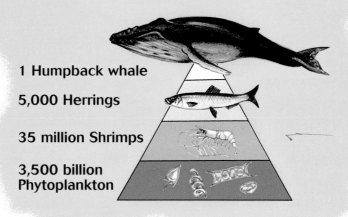

Ocean pyramid

A **pyramid of numbers** for the ocean might look like this one.

1 Humpback whale

5,000 Herrings

35 million Shrimps

3,500 billion Phytoplankton

Deep-sea features

In the depths of the ocean, it is dark and very cold. No plants can grow here because there is no sunlight for photosynthesis. As a result, food is scarce. Deep-sea animals must eat other animals or the remains of dead plants and animals that drift down from the surface. Many have special features to make the most of any food they find. Gulper eels, for example, have huge mouths and elastic stomachs for swallowing **prey** much bigger than themselves.

Did you know?

Sea cucumbers are **echinoderms** that live on the seabed and feed on tiny scraps of food. They can shoot out streams of **entrails,** or sticky guts, that entangle hungry attackers. The entrails regrow within a few weeks.

Seashores and Reefs

Twice a day, the sea rises and floods the shore, then ebbs, or falls away again. These changes in sea level are called tides. Most seashore animals time their search for food to low tide. The food is plentiful at that time.

Seaweeds

Like **phytoplankton,** seaweeds are a type of **algae.** They anchor themselves to rocks along the coast with a root-like **holdfast.** When the sea comes in, phytoplankton float near the surface to absorb sunlight for **photosynthesis.** Small animals, such as sea-snails, graze on seaweeds.

Shore birds

When the tide is out, wading birds such as curlews and oystercatchers gather to feed on the shore. Curlews probe the sand and mud for shellfish and worms with their long, curved beaks. Oystercatchers use their long, strong beaks to pry open clam and mussel shells.

Redshanks feed on the seashore.

Coral reefs

Almost a third of all the world's fish species live around coral reefs. Reefs are home to thousands of creatures, from brilliantly colored butterfly fish to enormous giant clams. Each creature has its own niche, or place, in the reef **ecosystem** and its own source of food.

Coral builders

Coral reefs are built by tiny polyps, which are related to jellyfish and sea anemones. Like sea anemones, coral polyps use stinging tentacles to stun or kill their **prey.** The polyps build stony, cup-like cases to protect their soft bodies. When the polyps die, their cases are left behind. Corals can grow only in shallow, sunny water. This is because they grow in partnership with algae, which need sunlight in order to photosynthesize.

A coral reef provides a home for many animals.

Coral feeders

Many animals feed on the coral itself. Parrot fish get their name from their sharp, parrot-like beaks, which are formed by their front teeth. The fish scrapes away at the hard coral, then uses another set of teeth to crush the coral.

Did you know?
Parts of the Great Barrier Reef in Australia are being eaten away by the crown-of-thorns starfish. The starfish grips a piece of coral in its arms, then pushes its stomach out over it. The starfish takes several hours to digest the coral. Then it pulls its stomach in and moves on.

Food Chains and You

What was your last meal? A pizza? A tuna fish sandwich? A bowl of cereal? Whatever you ate, it connects you to a food chain or to a larger food web. Human beings are usually considered to be **omnivores,** because we eat both plants and animals. Our ancestors were hunter-gatherers. They hunted wild animals for meat, and gathered plants. Luckily, we no longer have to go out hunting. We can buy all the food we need in the supermarket!

Fish is an important source of proteins and oils.

A balanced diet

To get all the **nutrients** and energy you need and to stay healthy, you need to eat foods from six major groups:

- Carbohydrates—for energy. Found in bread, rice, and cereals.
- Proteins—for growth and repair. Found in meat, fish, eggs, and beans.
- Fats—for energy and warmth. Found in milk, cheese, butter, and oils.
- Vitamins—for regulating chemical processes in your body. Found in fruit, vegetables, fish, and milk.
- Minerals—for healthy cells. Found in fish, vegetables, fruit, and milk.
- Fiber—for healthy digestion. Found in fruit, vegetables, whole-wheat bread, and bran.

Two food chains

If you eat a tuna fish sandwich, you are part of two food chains, one long and one short. In the first food chain, which supplied the tuna, you are the fourth consumer in the chain. In the second, which supplied the bread, you are the primary consumer.

1 **Phytoplankton** → **zooplankton** → small fish → tuna → you
2 Wheat (the wheat is made into bread) → you

Vegetarians and vegans

Some people choose not to eat meat. Vegetarians eat vegetables, fruit, nuts, legumes such as lentils and beans, and grains such as wheat. They do not eat meat or fish. Some vegetarians eat eggs and dairy products.

Vegans do not eat any animal products. This includes eggs, honey, and anything that may contain animal fat. Vegans are always primary **consumers.** Vegetarians are usually primary consumers, because they eat food that comes directly from plants. For example, the food chains for a salad with cheese in it would look like this:

1 Grass → cow (the cow's milk is made into cheese) → you
2 Salad vegetables → you

Cycles in Nature

In nature, nothing goes to waste. Everything is constantly being recycled and used again. When living things die, their bodies **decompose.** Other living things break them down into basic minerals and chemicals that plants can use to grow. In this way, the cycle begins again. **Recycling** is very important. If it did not happen, living creatures would run out of the things they need to grow.

Decomposers

Bacteria, **fungi**—shown in the picture, and some types of insects feed on the remains of animals and plants. They are called decomposers, and are found at every stage in every food chain. Decomposers break down dead plants and animals into **humus** and minerals in the

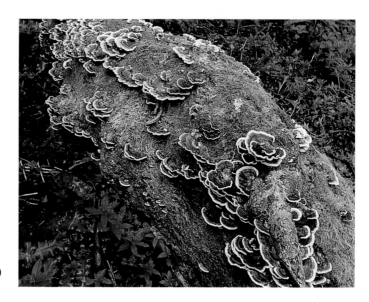

soil. As they do so, they not only obtain the energy they need to live but also enrich the soil so that plants can grow. Bacteria also release **carbon dioxide**, which can be used by plants for **photosynthesis.** Decomposers are often left out of food webs and **pyramids of numbers** because it is so difficult to count or show them.

Feeding fungi

Fungi are neither plants nor animals. They belong to a third **kingdom,** or group of living things. A fungus is made up of a mass of tiny threads called hyphae. The threads of hyphae branch over dead material, dissolve it, then soak it up. Fungi live on dead material such as dead leaves or rotting tree trunks. They are called **saprophytes.**

Carbon cycle

Carbon is one of the basic elements that make up all living things. This is how the carbon cycle works:

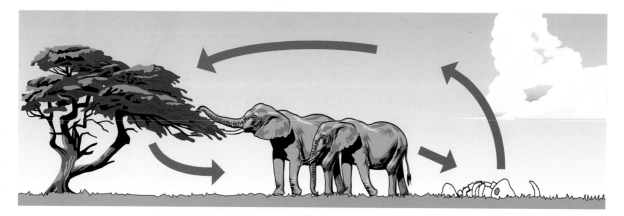

1. Carbon dioxide is released in the air.
2. Plants use carbon dioxide to photosynthesize and make food.
3. Animals eat plants and obtain carbon.
4. Animals use carbon from plants for energy and growth.
5. Animals produce waste and eventually die.
6. Decomposers feed on the dead plant and animal matter and release carbon dioxide into the air.

Nitrogen cycle

Living things also need **nitrogen** for growth. The basic nitrogen cycle is quite simple:

1 Green plants take in **nitrates** from the soil.
2 Plants use nitrogen in these nitrates to build **proteins** for growth.
3 When plants die, decomposers break the proteins down into **ammonium** compounds.
4 Animals also eat the plants.
5 Animal waste and dead animal carcasses are broken down into ammonium compounds.
6 Bacteria in the soil converts the ammonium back into nitrates.

Upsetting the Balance

In a food chain or web, the balance between **producers** and **consumers** is a delicate one if there is going to be enough to eat. The balance can be easily upset by natural and human means. If something happens to one of the links in the chain, disaster can strike all the others. For example, in a simple pond food chain, herons eat frogs that eat insects that eat plants. If the frogs were to die off, the herons would not have enough to eat. Without frogs to eat them, the number of insects would dramatically increase. However, there might not be enough plants to feed all of the insects.

When things go wrong

Poisons build up as they pass along a food chain. For example, DDT is a chemical once widely sprayed on crops to kill insects. During the 1960s, scientists noticed a decrease in the number of certain birds of **prey,** such as ospreys. They found that the ospreys contained large amounts of DDT. The birds were poisoned because the DDT sprayed on the crops was not **biodegradable.** It built up in the soil, then washed into rivers and seas. There, it was taken up by **phytoplankton,** which were eaten by **zooplankton,** then fish, then ospreys.

This osprey is feeding its young.

Poisoned shellfish

The metal mercury is another poison that can enter the food chain with deadly consequences. In 1952, a chemical factory in Japan leaked mercury into the sea. More than 100 people died, and thousands more were paralyzed by eating shellfish poisoned by the mercury.

Competition for food

The more food that is available to an animal, the better its chance of survival. But the more animals species there are competing for a food source, the smaller the populations of those species will be. For example, if two types of animals are competing for grass, some will starve because less food is available for each of them.

Did you know?

Lemmings are small rodents from Norway. They feed on grasses, mosses, and shrubs. They breed very quickly, putting great pressure on their food supplies. Every four years, there is a lemming population explosion. The animals leave their homes by the thousands to search for more food. In their hurry, many fall over cliffs or drown in the sea. This reduces the number of lemmings to a manageable size, and life for the lemmings returns to normal—at least for a while!

Conclusion

All living things need regular supplies of food to fuel their bodies, to help them to grow, and to keep them in good working order. In a particular **ecosystem**, food passes from plant to animal, and from animal to animal, along a food chain. Each plant and animal is a vital link in the chain. Human beings, too, are part of many different food chains and webs. Think about what you have eaten in the last few days. How many food chains have you been part of?

Glossary

algae   one-celled plant found in both saltwater and freshwater

ammonium   chemical made by mixing nitrogen and other chemicals

bacteria   living thing, only visible under a microscope, found almost everywhere on Earth

baleen plate   bone-like structure in a whale's mouth that it uses to filter out food from the water

biodegradable   able to rot or break down naturally

biomass   total amount of each individual type of living thing in a food chain

boreal   type of forest that grows in a band across the far north, or polar, region of the world

browser   animal that eats the leaves of trees or bushes

camouflaged   blending in with the surroundings, usually by shape, color, or pattern, to be less noticeable

carbon   vitally important chemical element found in the bodies of all living things

carbon dioxide   gas that living things breathe out during respiration; plants use carbon dioxide in photosynthesis

carcass   dead body of an animal

carnivore   animal that eats only the meat of other animals

chlorophyll   green coloring found inside plants that absorbs energy from sunlight for use in photosynthesis

community   plants and animals that live together in a certain habitat

coniferous   type of tree that produces cones

consumer   in a food chain, animal that feeds directly on plants, or indirectly on them by eating other animals

deciduous   trees and plants that regularly shed their leaves

decompose   to rot or break down

echinoderm   invertebrate animal that lives in the sea, such as starfish, sea urchins, and sea cucumbers

ecosystem   community of animals and plants and the habitat in which they live

entrails   animal innards or bowels

evergreen   type of tree that keeps its leaves all year round

forage   to wander in search of food

fungi   large kingdom of living things that obtain energy by decaying and decomposing other living things

glucose   simple sugar that plants store as food

grassland   large, open, flat area covered in grasses and low bushes

grazer   animal that eats or grazes on grass

habitat   distinctive type of place or surroundings, such as a woodland, mountain top, grassland, pond, or seashore

herbivore   animal that eats only plants

hibernate/hibernation   when an animal's body functions slow down to allow it to survive periods of intense cold and lack of food

holdfast   part by which a plant clings to a flat surface

humus   rich, dark material made from the decomposing bodies of dead plants and animals

invertebrate   animal that does not have a backbone or skeleton in its body

larva   young form of insect that looks very different from adults—plural is larvae

mass   number of living things in a contained space

nitrate   form of nitrogen found in the soil

nitrogen   colorless gas that living things need for growth

nutrient   substance needed by a living thing for its growth, development, and survival

omnivore   animal that eats both plants and animals

oxygen   gas that all living things need to take in to survive

photosynthesis   process by which green plants use energy from carbon dioxide and water, using energy from sunlight absorbed by their chlorophyll

phytoplankton   microscopic, single-celled plants that live in the sea and form the start of the ocean food chain

pigment   natural coloring or dye

predator   animal that hunts and kills other animals for food

prey   animals that are hunted and eaten by other animals

proboscis   long, hollow tube, like a tongue, through which butterflies drink nectar and water

producer   in a food chain, the green plants that make their own food by photosynthesis, and start every food chain

protein   chemical substance that living things need for growth

pyramid of biomass   diagram that shows the total amount of each living thing in a food chain in terms of its mass

pyramid of numbers   diagram that shows the total number of each living thing in a food chain

recycling   process by which materials are used again and again

saprophyte   living thing that feeds on dead or decaying plant matter

scavenger   animal that feeds on the dead bodies of other animals or plants

shoal   large number of fish that swim and live together

species   group of living things that look similar to each other and can breed together, but that cannot breed with other living things

temperate   having cold winters and warm summers

zooplankton   tiny sea animals that graze on phytoplankton

More Books to Read

Barre, Michel. *Animals and the Quest for Food.* Milwaukee, Wis.: Gareth Stevens Publishing, 1998.

McKinney, Barbara. *Pass the Energy, Please.* Nevada City, Cal.: Dawn Publications, 2000.

Silverstein, Alvin, Virginia Silverstein, and Laura Silverstein Nunn. *Food Chains.* Brookfield, Conn.: Millbrook Press, 1998.

Index